Jump Straight Up

Late New Poems

Jarold Ramsey

A Publication of The Poetry Box®

Poems ©2023 Jarold Ramsey
All rights reserved.

Editing & Book Design by Shawn Aveningo Sanders
Cover Design by Shawn Aveningo Sanders
Cover Photograph is of Les Steers, high jumper for University of
　　Oregon, and longtime World Record holder, while practicing
　　at Hayward Field in Spring, 1941. Photo provided by Jarold Ramsey
　　(source & photographer indeterminable)
Author Photo (on p. 45) by Dorothy Ramsey

No part of this book may be republished without permission
from the author, except in the case of brief quotations
embodied in critical essays, epigraphs, reviews and articles,
or publisher/author's marketing collateral.

ISBN: 978-1-956285-44-4
Printed in the United States of America.
Wholesale distribution via Ingram.

Published by The Poetry Box®, November 2023
Portland, Oregon
https://thepoetrybox.com

To Our Grandchildren

~ Contents ~

9	The Ballad of Whistling Smith
11	Pop and Fritz Kreisler
12	The Hole through Mt. Jefferson
14	Coyote's Epilogue to the Telling
15	Time Capsule
16	The Quarrel
17	For W.S. Merwin
18	The Aeolian Harp Makes a Comeback
20	The Plumb-Bob Heart
21	Beyond Gravitas
22	Flusterings
23	Gratitude
24	Interspecies
25	Wolf Spider
26	Maeve and the Finch
27	Slime Mold Dream
30	Ike and His Whangdoodle
32	Similitude
33	Transit of Venus
34	Two Mornings in Early June
35	Dixieland Treadmill
37	Report from an Island
38	Jump Straight Up
41	Acknowledgments
43	Early Praise
45	About the Author

Jump Straight Up

The Ballad of Whistling Smith

Whistling Smith, oh Whistling Smith,
   can you hear him whistling in the snow
way down, way down in John Brown Canyon
   and the air at forty below?

East of the mountains, out on the range,
   you hear tales of the Blizzard of Eighty-Four—
four days and nights of heavy snow
   and Jack Frost went on a tear

and dropped the mercury to forty below
   and the snow was up to your chest!
Whistling Smith was Boyce's man
   and for herding sheep he was the best.

At the head of the canyon, he had a shack
   with a rimrock fireplace quite amazing
while it stood, where he ate and slept
   when not with his sheep at their grazing.

A quiet man, but he was always whistling,
   they say, both day and night,
and the flocks in his care were calm and easy
   hearing him, out of sight.

No one remembers the tunes he whistled.
   But you're welcome to guess if you like—
"Yankee Doodle," and "Shenandoah,"
   and "Dixie," and "Sweet Betsy from Pike"?

Late in the day the blizzard began
   with his sheep in the canyon, he tried
to hike down for a look, but the going was tough,
   so he came home, and went inside.

The next day at noon, with the snow still falling,
    for his boss he left a short screed—
"Am heading down to check on the critters.
    Will stay at Brown's if I need."

So he started down, and whistled as he struggled,
    breasting the snow for a mile
or more, finding no trace of the sheep,
    until he stopped for a while

under a sheltering juniper tree
    to ease his pounding heart,
and find what little warmth he could
    before the day turned to dark.

When the snow had finally melted away
    in early March, they found
him there, and his mortal remains were attested
    by his friend and neighbor John Brown.

The sheep had mostly died, and their wool
    you could see it for years in clumps.
His bones were buried in a canyonside field
    until a homesteader plowed them up.

Whistling Smith, oh Whistling Smith,
    can you hear him whistling in the snow,
way down, way down in John Brown Canyon
    and the air at forty below?

Pop and Fritz Kreisler

My grandpa came from a musical family
in the hills of east Tennessee, out to Oregon,
"The Mendenhall Boys" his older brothers,
all accomplished pickers and strummers;
their grandmother Keirsey herself a pipe-smoking
fiddler, and Pop grew up playing her heirloom fiddle
until someone smashed it in a runaway,
and he bought a replacement, and I found the saved pieces
years later, and cobbled it together, but not for playing.

Everywhere in our homestead country, Lamonta,
Culver, Opal City, "Heelstring Nation,"
he played for the all-night dances, his brother Walt
on the banjo, Bill Barber on the bones, and when
she learned to chord, my mother would "second" for them
on the piano, as they galloped through
"Cotton-Eyed Joe," "Money Musk,"
"Devil's Dream," reeling it out by ear and heart,
until Pop grunted "Change!" and she would change
the key, and off they'd go, higher, faster.

Seventy years later people who danced those nights
still recalled his playing—"Nobody fiddled like Joe!"
His wife Ella wasn't musical, but I fancy
when he played, she was his music.
When she died at 44, he hung up his fiddle.
But thereafter never missed a radio broadcast
by his age-mate and fellow virtuoso Fritz Kreisler.
I know all the stories,
but I never heard him play.

The Hole through Mt. Jefferson

Once, once only, home from climbing
Mt. Jefferson, looking back at dusk
to where I'd been of late in a pleasant zone
of duress and danger, I saw a bnlliant spark
ignite in that dense shadow, somewhere around
the head of Whitewater Glacier, incandescent,
as if about to blaze out to supernova.
Instead, before I could breathe again it vanished,
leaving the mountain blacker than before.
What had I seen there twenty miles to the west?
The casual impact of an airplane on the glacier?
Some fallen brother climber, shooting a flare?
Something extra-terrestrial, intelligent, meant for me?
Next day, no one was missing, that night
no spark. I told no one. All I took
with me henceforth was that bare illumination.

Some of my best friends live west of the mountains,
but I live over here, just east of the range
that divides our state culturally like a nine-wire fence.
And it's a drag, sometimes, to try to explain
Madras, or Fossil, to *The Oregonian* (and vice-versa),
and four years of college in the valley of the Willamette
could not erase the utter strangeness of watching
sunrise over the Cascade Mountains. East
and west—it's a reprehensible trick of our thoughts,
the slippery way one such dichotomy runs
into all the others, digging a binary
groove in the floor of the brain—north and south,
wet and dry, "blue" and "red", Mars
and Venus, flesh and spirit, here and there....
Plato's curse! And maybe the music of our world
is too rich to be broadcast and heard on a digital
system, all lilts and airs abstracted to ones and zeroes.

Driving over the Santiam Pass, on either
side of the divide, the eyes of roadside deer
and bobcats gleam in my headlights about the same.
What they know is the immediate way they're going.
Likewise, Old Man Coyote, equally at home
on the outskirts of Simnasho and Newberg,
forever meddling with every polarity
he meets, playing both sides against the middle
with omnivorous gusto, our native mediator,
Coyote—let's draft him to run for Governor
of Oregon, on the "Trickster Unity" ticket!

That spark on Mt. Jefferson—what if, that once,
the mountain relented a little, allowing a crack
or fissure to run clean through its nitty-gritty,
and a momentary ray of valley sunset
escaped over here, and I saw it? What if
it happens again, at dawn, and some dairyman
in Stayton or Sublimity looking east sees a flash
on the shadow mountain? And then suppose,
despite all, the fissure floods with Oregon sunlight?
If we found it, we could signal to each other!
On both sides, let there be a sharing of light.

Coyote's Epilogue to the Telling

~for Mrs. Victoria Howard and Melville Jacobs

And now, let us leave this storyteller
and the disjointed story he has made of us,
let us leave the fireside, the lodge of drowsy people
who inherit this world once wholly ours:
let us separate, my friends, once more, becoming
birds of the great air
fish of the endless waters
lithe animals of the forest
nimble animals of the mountains—
and I, Coyote, last to go my way,
reality's handyman, look back and grin
like a dog to think these poor listening fools,
these people who were always "coming soon,"
the story-man himself,
all will rise, and go, and burrow
deep into the winter night, full of beginnings,
their world no more perfect than before
but such as it is
enabled, empowered with our names.

The Time Capsule

Is there no end to the excavation of childhood? No—the shameless archaeologist will do anything, dig anywhere, for a shard or a shred, an abject or an ort of my legendary forebear the Happy Boy. Of him and his earthy cult, the Museum demands always more artifacts.

But vaguely under a backyard lawn there lies, at a mythical depth, a treasure-trove, a Sutton Hoo of who I was once upon a time; no electronic instrument can find it. All one summer, the Boy kept busy in secret burying tokens of his life—toys, gimcracks, coded messages—in a wide-mouth mason jar with a glass lid. He'd read somewhere about Masonic corner-stones full of news of the past for eager posterity, and once a month, if not before, bored with the present, he would dig up the jar and scrutinize the contents for evidence that he'd made it to the future.

The signs in the jar were always doubtful, and after a little re-arrangement of items he would bury it all over again. At last came a day when he forgot—and *that* was the future, but he missed it, and went blundering on. Most of a lifetime later, the jar is still there, hermetic in the soil, its childish contents undisturbed, and by now all turned to bright filagree of gold.

How do I know all this? I am the genie of the jar.

The Quarrel

~for JRR (1932-2020)

Mac, why was it
after six days off-trail
from Hetch Hetchy to Branigan Lakes,
confronting those miseries and wonders with one mind—
the heat the outlaw bears lurking for grub
the golden trout impossible to catch
impossible to leave alone in their indigo waters
the honest-to-God wolf you saw at the high camp
extinct since 1916 but I believe you
the spindle-shaped junipers somehow screwed alive
into the golden monolith that is Yosemite
all those perfections of rock, blue air, and light
and higher, always higher,
one mind between us, brother, up and back—
why then, down in the Valley,
restored to telephones, traffic, and deadlines,
did we fly off our handles without warning
raging at each other in the little pickup cab
like a soap opera, petty grievances
unfolding clear back to the bloody quick of childhood
leaving us both shaken, distracted, and sorry
all the way down to Modesto and beyond...
why? I suppose it was something bound to happen,
as divers pulled up too quickly get the bends
embolisms of joy bursting the narrow vessels—
We are very different, brother,
and we go our own ways much of the time
but having long ago once re-named each other
as adolescents, "Mac," God knows why,
we still answer, just we two,
to that same unchristened name, *Mac.*

For W.S. Merwin
   (1927-2019)

It must have been the year we lived
on Vancouver Island, and you stopped over
on the way back from Maui into your world at large.
For once, I remember, there was time and leisure
to shake down with each other—we still in flight
from our nation's evil war, but resigned
to go home to it; you full of Maui
and wonderful prospects of ravaged palm-tree groves
to be restored, and an old shack that might be made
livable again, like your beloved farmhouse in France.
Who would help you, we wondered.
But what I most dearly remember
was walking back up the hill to our rented house
from the village of Oak Bay, and looking back
to see you in communion with Sophie and John,
a child of ours gaily held
in each of your hands.

The Aeolian Harp Makes a Comeback

~for Ursula LeGuin (1929-2018)

At one time, if you aspired to be a poet, or a seer,
you needed one of these—Coleridge had one, famously,
as did Emerson, and Thoreau, and for the German
Romantics they were as essential as ruined castles and milkmaids.
And lately, a dear friend has told me how
she'd been haunted for years after hearing one.

So, finding no kits or even detailed plans,
I took in hand thin plywood, sandpaper, glue,
assorted tools and clamps, tuning pegs,
and what became a lifetime supply of mono-
filament nylon fishing line of different
weights, and cobbled the thing together ad hoc.

Then laid it out on a window ledge, like an apple
pie just out of the oven, and waited,
hopelessly, for the north wind to come around.
When it came, at first there was no music, deafeningly,
but then, a thin pure note, as if keening inside
my head like tinnitus, then turning vibrato,
then joined by another insistent note, an octave
lower, then a third in perfect harmony with these;
then a tone disharmonious with the others, raucous,
as if sent to stir up discord and mischief in the choir;
and then, abrupt silence, although the breeze
was still blowing outside; and then a new recital
in a different key, louder than before—
and then silence again, and so on, leaving
me all ears that day, nothing but ears.

Oh Boreas, and Zephyrus, and also Eurus and Notus,
you tricky skulkers around classical corners,
who would have guessed that out here in the boonies
your workaday breezes could carry such magical voices?
And dear friend of the air, what are you hearing now,
wherever you are, out there in the four winds?

The Plumb-Bob Heart

~for Bob Berky

"Born in a barn?"
When they sneer at our antics
you and I know it's a compliment, man.
Where else, when the morning sun
crashes the gate in a thousand planks
of dancing light, and the moldy hay
begins to warm again to its dream of the field.

So I see you come out at dawn to the mow
to practice out-clowning the tittering owls on a rope
you've tuned, I hope, to the key of "G"—
Gravity, Grace, and Vertigo.
Such tricks and turns of the aerial feet!
First mincing a long inch from the wall—
then a rush, and a skip, and a teetering stand,
all striped with light, astonished the way
ridiculous gestures bear you up,
and how easy it is in transit, wearing
your plumb-bob heart in the ball of your foot.

From my knothole, friend, I look to see you yet,
walking your sunbeam rope right out of the barn
with the whole wide upturned world
your only net.

Beyond Gravitas

They said it couldn't be done
or more precisely he shouldn't try it
—not, surely, at three score and fifteen!
—not, please, with your bionic hip!
But what was he to do, with his grandchild,
who had been taking Circus lessons,
showing off a repertory of stunts
but couldn't manage a headstand?

Head to the floor, hands pressing downward for balance,
elbows akimbo, knees hoisted and briefly
cradled on the elbows, then legs slowly lifted,
straightened, wavering, but marking time
beyond gravitas over his pulsing head.

There now kiddo, that's how it's done,
said grandpa the old show-off,
seeing spots as he clambered down to earth,
already thinking about the next family lesson,
with Leo, Harper, Samantha, Maddy, and Willa,
all conspired on the floor with him,
all dangerously upside down for love,
twelve legs straight up waving like saplings,
reaching for the leaves and the birds!

Flusterings

The unaccountable grandpa enters the room.
As he approaches where his waggish granddaughter
sits, humped in a brown-haired study
with her iPad, which the old-fashioned grandpa does not favor,
an irresistible impulse tickles his brain and he reaches out
one gnarly hand and roughly, rudely flusters
the digitalized granddaughter's hair,
mussing it round and round and every which way.
The imperturbable granddaughter giggles
but does not look up from the glow of her iPad séance.

But that night, while the ruminant grandpa is reading
in his chair, the rascally granddaughter sidles up
and strikes with both hands, ruffling the defenseless
grandpa's grey locks as if a heap of wool,
leaving him a mane like Harpo's, or Brian May's.

O neighbors, take heed!
The unanimous grandpa and granddaughter
are now running amok through this stodgy neighborhood,
flustering every head of hair they can find
for all they are worth, their eyes ablaze, beware!

Gratitude

The bumblebee's flight plan

is anything but random between the apple blossoms.

Next winter, when I'm eating an apple

from this old tree

will I remember to be grateful?

Interspecies

Where have you been? you ask,
and I reply, Out with the vegetables,
trying to negotiate with the young tendrils
of the pea-vines, as to why they steadfastly refuse
to curl around the strings I've provided them with between
the customary poles, the way I want them to, now.
They reach out with their delicate tips already hooked
as if eager to latch on, but blindly miss the strings.
When I very gently attempt to wind them on,
they promptly unwind themselves, and dangle aimlessly.
I wonder if peas-tendrils curl in this hemisphere
clockwise, or counterclockwise? In Australia, the reverse?
Sometimes after my meddling they connect with each other
in a useless tangle. When, on their own, they succeed
in grabbing the string, it is, I will admit,
an elegant achievement, like a fine bit of stitchery.
But all this seems to leave me baffled and sulky,
like a child who feels rejected by its mother,
left out, a creature of no consequence.

Wolf Spider

Every morning, for almost a week now,
a wolf spider has rappelled
on an invisible strand out of its spinneret
from the ceiling of our bathroom while I'm shaving,
to dangle there, eye to eye,
so close I can see its trim forelegs
and the rows of those multiple black eyes
sizing me up—for what?

I've always admired how its kind, *Lycosidae*,
on the ground look more like animals than spiders,
like tiny wolves, in fact—bewhiskered head and body
and legs, all in a comely functional unit,
not creepily strung out like a black widow spider.
And, whether hunting or escaping, how they can jump,
forward, backward, sideways!

But now, this one has seen fit to winch itself
down alongside my whiskery face, not to escape,
or surely not to hunt—maybe just to hang out
in this steamy bathroom with this odd vertical
shifty-eyed creature, before going on its web-less way,
and I on mine.

Maeve and the Finch

There was a young cat (her name was Maeve)
who was totally black, pantherish, and brave,
as befits a namesake of the Queen of Connacht,
the most willful monarch who ever walked.

Maeve (the cat) liked to perch on the back
of a chair near a window, on which was stuck
on the outside a tray that was kept full of seeds
of millet and thistles and other weeds

which drew the birds, in eager congregation,
while the cat watched in silent agitation,
her tail lashing and now and then extending
a paw, as if a signal intending,

which the birds ignored, and came and departed
while Maeve lurked inside, wild-hearted,
yearning for prey, if only a morsel,
a bit of a sparrow, be it ventral or dorsal—

but at length she noticed there on the tray
a particular finch, which came day after day,
and at times just perched there, eyeing the cat,
and cocked its head, as if wanting to chat;

and more than once pecked at the glass, as if saying
"Hey there, Cat, I know what you're weighing,
but given this window, on which much depends,
I ask you up front, why can't we be friends?"

And you know, all that winter, the cat and the bird
communed through the window with nary a word,
but they chatted and gossiped through wind, rain, and thunder—
what was it about? Don't you wonder?

The Slime Mold Dream

He came upon it as he was skirting a fen in the Mt. Hood National Forest, east of Bear Springs. The color of it—an astonishing psychedelic yellow—caught his eye. It was just off the trail, on a big fallen log, maybe three feet off the ground. Except for the color, it looked like a garden slug, about four inches long, with no visible feelers or horns. However it had gotten itself up on the fallen log, it was creeping along, a faint trail of drying ooze marking its progress so far, and clearly, although almost imperceptibly, it was moving along the horizontal log.

Must be a slime mold, he thought, remembering network news coverage of alarms in Texas about the sudden appearance of great blobs of bright yellow goo in suburban backyards—OUTER SPACE INVADERS IN HOUSTON? No, authorities explained—just ordinary slime molds. And, as if proof of this non-explanation, they were gone the next morning.

But this must be a different kind of slime mold, he decided. Looking down at it, he considered gathering it up and taking it home for observation—the grandkids would be intrigued by it. But he didn't have a suitable container, and carrying it in his bare hands to the car didn't seem like a good option, for it, or for him.

So he contented himself by photographing it, and enjoying its "dayglo" color. When he poked it with a stick, it gave no response, except for a little ooze at the contact point. All the while, he noted, it had continued its infinitely slow progress along the tree-trunk.

At home that night, he had a dream. He was back in the woods, and the slime mold was talking to him from the log, as if in his own voice. "We greet you in the name of our kind! We have learned that the only way to communicate with your kind is through dreams, and through that medium we have ascertained that your scientists have chosen to call us "cellular slime molds." We regret that the rather derogatory terms 'slime' and 'mold' have been imposed on us, because we are certainly not "moldy," and in a strict sense we are not "slimy" either. But so be it, and we do appreciate it that some of your scientists have given up their long futile effort to classify our kind as either animals, or plants—specifically fungi! We applaud their establishment of a third category for us and our relatives—the Protists, which seems to indicate that you are at last recognizing that we are neither animals nor plants—and that we appeared on this earth very early, and have managed to carry on with our distinctive way of life all that time, despite more challenges than your short history comprehends.

In sum: we are one-celled fellow creatures that you have named *amoebae*, meaning that we begin our lives on the forest floor as individual organisms, and subsist there until food becomes scarce, and the Great Signal comes that calls us all together, millions of us in a mobile assembly like what you found on the log this morning, all of us retaining our cellular identities, but united in the one purpose of reproduction. Soon after you left us, we advanced to the right place on the log, where volunteers of us transformed into 'fruiting bodies' as you call them, and then an honored few of us became spores, and blew off in the winds of the forest to create new generations of our kind.

We assume that your kind also somehow reproduces itself periodically, though apparently not through great transformative assemblies like ours. Whatever it is that initiates and signals the reproductive motive in you, we want to believe that, with you as with us, it is based on a primal collective aim to carry on, to keep alive. Our kind has a proverb: 'We are always beginning, and never ending.'

If we share this aim, then we urge you to live and act in the world we occupy together with more respect and considerate attention.

From our admittedly remote and low-level perspective, your kind appears to serve only itself. If our woods are cut down and dry up, or burn, is it not your loss as well as ours, who were living here long before your kind came?

The fact that you chose not to remove us from the log today, thus allowing us to carry on with our reproductive mission, shows, perhaps, restraint and consideration on your part, and it has led to this attempt at interspecies communication. We will not attempt to speak to you again. But in conclusion, we know that your scientists have discovered and are making extensive laboratory use of the fact that we are very fond of your food, *oatmeal* . Perhaps it is the first known gift from your kind to ours. So, when you sit down to your next dish of cooked oatmeal, think of us. Farewell."

Ike and His Whangdoodle

Old Ike lived way up the creek, and whittled incessantly, morning noon and night, and in between—pinewood bears and dogs, and interlocking chains, and spindly human figures that vaguely resembled but did not flatter his neighbors along the creek. But then Ike launched into a series of clever "action" figures operated by the wind powering a little windmill whatsis at one end—pecking chickens, a man chopping wood, two bicyclists pedaling along, a high-kicking dancing man, a pair of loose-jointed prize-fighters whaling away at one another as long as the wind blew, out where he displayed them, one by one on the mailbox by the road. Folks thought they were clever, and he may have even sold a few of them to tourists who came by in search of local color.

Maybe it was the profit motive that inspired his ultimate whangdoodle, but I doubt it. All we knew was that one morning, on his mailbox, there appeared a wooden couple making love, stiffly but energetically whenever a breeze came up—the figures lovingly carved out of pine or maybe basswood, as anatomically correct as need be, their loose-jointed action ingeniously driven by wires and linkages and crankshafts connected to the little windmill, the whole thing on show out there in front of his shack for all the world to see—which it did, for over a week, beginning with the mailman, and the school bus driver and his wide-eyed passengers, and the Watkins-McNess salesman, who told others on his route about Ike's latest wonder, and so whole crowds came out from town to gawk, especially when the wind was blowing; and soon there were Letters to the Editor, and denunciations by preachers to their congregations, and a TV station in the next county was reportedly about to send out a crew.

But one night the wind blew up a gale, and after an hour or so of increasingly out of control lovemaking, the whole thing simply flew apart, and all that was left on the mailbox the next morning were a few wires and linkages, and two pairs of articulated legs. And though there were some around here who urged Ike to reconstruct his pair of mechanical lovebirds, and maybe even build a whole orgy of them, he never did, and all he ever said about his creation was, "The wind made me do it."

Similitude

When I found you today
unawares, in a crowd of strangers
it was like
sneaking through deep timber
no trail
lost in perpetual blowdown
weary of shadow and hillside drab as a suburb
thirsty for glimpses of skyline over the stifling fir tops.
And then, cresting a ridge,
off to the west a thinning of branches
a glimmer of space
the sky turning blue turning over something beneath—
walking out of the woods at the very brink
of a meadow of water
everything good in this part of the world opens up:
the mountain lake
you in that crowd

Transit of Venus

We were never more punctual, were we—
not for any transatlantic flight, not for our own wedding,
knowing that the orbits of heaven do not wait for anything.
Beforehand we positioned the telescope, tracked
it on the afternoon sun ablaze in a cloudless sky,
adjusted the projection screen so that the sun's
disc filled it with incandescent light.
Then looked at the disc, looked at the screen, looked
at the clock until mere seconds remained, then none,
and still the sun sailed on, immaculate, with centuries
of expert calculations and our own feeble grasp
of the infinite hanging in the balance—

until you cried *There! Look there!*
and together, rapt, we saw a tiny black
inward bulge in the right edge of the solar
disc, and as we held one breath between us,
it broke free and became its own orb,
now riding serenely across that immense
wheel of light, taking us along,
only the two of us in transit,
no longer earthbound.

Two Mornings in Early June

I.

When you say of the young robins strutting and posturing
over the back lawn, "Oh, they're so full of it!"
what are they so full of, do you think?
Worms in the grass, and the prospect of worms?
Maybe, too, something in the late spring air
and light this very morning? Whatever it is,
I can see it in the glint of your eyes
this very morning.

II.

When the young cock meadowlark
reared back on his fencepost, opened his beak,
and premiered his gallant mating song, blessing
the pastures, the cows and calves, the momentary
spring air as he sang—
    was it just yesterday, me standing there with my old man's ears?
    Or was it yesterday, when I was sixteen?
    Or maybe, for a moment somehow
it was both?

Dixieland Treadmill

Dear Louis, Maestro—so it's come to this:
I'm listening to you and the Hot Fives and Sevens
on a cheapo CD boombox blaring behind me
over the roar and squeal of this goddam treadmill
which I'm trying to keep up with as it tries its mechanical
best to run me back, back, and onto the floor,
like the last car off an assembly line.

Is this what "struttin' with some barbecue" must come to,
finally, the end of all our "stop-time" capering
down Bourbon Street in a swelling throng, emptying
every bar we pass? Still, Maestro,
we must try to keep dancing to your irresistible beat
as we did fifty-plus years ago at a college prom,
only you and Ella were so ravishing that night
most of us just stood around to drink it in,
until you grabbed the mike and growled, "What's wrong
with you young folks—why ain't you *dancin'*?
That's why we're up here *playin'*, you dig me?"
So we danced, perforce, and you beamed your approval all evening
like a searchlight.

                        Promenade gives way to treadmill,
fancy footwork to ataxia,
a segue not devoutly to be wished,
Louis, and I confess I've tried other
musical inspirations for these workouts:
Scott Joplin's ragtimes for one (too sprightly),
Sousa's marches for another (very uplifting,
but my cause is neither military nor patriotic).
And so, I'm much beholden to have you
and Ory, and Bechet, and Briggs, and the brothers Dodds,
and all your immortal sidemen on hand to carry
me forward aerobically on wings of song, so to speak,

even your brief vocalist before Lil, May Alix,
and her one great line, "I just want somebody who wants
me to play!" Sweetie, don't we all.

Trouble is, at this stage our good angels all counsel
something called fitness over play. What a drag.
Would you have jammed all night for "fitness," Maestro?
If I can last another quarter mile on this contraption
I will reach your sublime "Potato Head Blues," and then
"It's the Last Time," and maybe stop all this "wringin'
and twistin' motha, cause I ain't goin' no further!"
But while there's music playing, I'm bold to invite you
to join me on this endless un-conveying belt,
where we can bounce along together, steadying
each other arm in arm, unless you want
to bring your horn along and try some riffs
over the top as we go? Where we're going
really doesn't matter, whether forward
or backward or merely marking time
as long as we're going in such style!

Report from an Island

Lately, we've been living on an island—
a small island, almost circular, in a great river.
Which river, we're not sure, but clearly one of the great ones,
judging from how dim its banks are, almost invisible from here.
The house is familiar, and comfortable, with everything we need
ready to hand; but who built it, and who holds the title,
we don't know. "Not to worry!" we tell each other.

There are boats and even big ships on the river, but they sail
straight by, and out of sight downstream, and we
don't pay them much attention. Instead,
we attend to what's nearby, now, like the stars tonight,
and the shed snakeskin we found on the path this morning—
a brief wonder, but we probably won't keep it.
Moment by new moment, we have each other as we are,
after all the years, and it is enough for now.

Is someone coming for us, we wonder sometimes,
but if so it's not on the calendar,
which is marked up with other people's birthdays and memorials.
"Not to worry!" we tell each other.

Jump Straight Up

~on a photo of Les Steers high jumping

In late spring 1941, at Hayward Field,
there he is forever levitated
in the utter perfection of his leap,
laid out mid-air in the classic "Western Roll,"
his legs exactly parallel over the bar,
but his arms and hands relaxed in flight,
and his face impassive, as if daydreaming
seven feet up in the mild spring air
of Eugene, Oregon, as it was then.

In the background, earthbound bystanders
keenly attend his flight, with legs askew to keep
him up with body English. Beyond them,
under the young athlete aloft,
looking north, the way the weather of history generally
flows, you might see if you squint
till it hurts what's coming for this moment and its company—
Pearl Harbor, and Buchenwald, and Normandy,
and Hiroshima, and Heartbreak Ridge, and My Lai,
and Nine-Eleven, and Sandy Hook, and COVID,
and Mariupol, and so on, and so on, and so on . . . .

But look! Here is our jumper still transfixed in the air
by the beauty of his strength and will,
showing how important it is to jump
when we can, when we will, not just forward, or backward,
or sideways, but jump straight up,
free of the gravity of time.

Acknowledgments

With gratitude to the editors of the following anthologies and periodicals, where these poems first appeared:

"The Ballad of Whistling Smith," in *THE AGATE*, Spring 2023

"The Hole through Mt. Jefferson," in *These Mountains that Divide Us: an East/West Dialogue Poem*, ed. Jack Lorts (Traprock Books, 2011)

"Coyote's Epilogue to the Telling," in *The Telling of the World*, ed. W.S. Penn (New York: Stewart Tabori, and Chang, 1996)

"Dixieland Treadmill," in *Brilliant Corners: a Journal of Jazz and Literature* (Winter 2016, Vol. 21, No. 1)

Early Praise

A descendent of strummers and pickers and fiddlers, the compiler and editor of the justly famous *Coyote Was Going There* (his anthology of Oregon Indian Literature), Jarold Ramsey now gives us this welcome book of "new late poems." Whether it's with elegies or tributes, Ramsey prompts us toward joy, urging us to "jump straight up, / free of the gravity of time." Like Old Man Coyote "forever meddling with every polarity / he meets," this wise, spirited, buoying voice defies dichotomies and denies divisions. When Ramsey asserts "On both sides, let there be a sharing of light," we say a grateful "Amen." Jarold Ramsey is an Oregon treasure.

—Paulann Petersen, author of *My Kindred*

Robert Frost remarked that a poem begins in delight and ends in wisdom. Jarold Ramsey's "new late poems" abound with both. Walk these pages and meet the Happy Boy, the granddad standing on his head, elegies to friends and peers, love poems of long marriage, an ode to Satchmo conceived on a treadmill, an Aeolian harp, a curious wolf spider, and a slime mold that talks. *Jump Straight Up* is a buoyantly beautiful report from a Northwest master at age 85.

—John Daniel, author of *Gifted*
and *Lighted Distances: Four Seasons on Goodlow Rim*

How often do you get to read poems firmly planted in a boyish elderhood, alive to past wonders yet rueful over losses rich and uncountable? This book delivers rich devotions to local antics and timeless questions, to natural wonders and human resonance with family neighbor, community character, companionable spider, meadowlark, coyote, amoeba. Long a student of story from Native myth to Shakespeare, Ramsey here delivers accounts of history, local lore, love for kinfolk, and yearning to understand the changes carrying us all along, richly in need of poems just like these.

—Kim Stafford, author of *Singer Come from Afar*

About the Author

Jarold Ramsey grew up on a ranch north of Madras, Oregon, and earned a BA in English from the University of Oregon, and a PhD in English Literature from the University of Washington. For nearly thirty years he taught Shakespeare, Modern Poetry, Creative Writing, and Native American Literature at the University of Rochester in New York State. He and his wife Dorothy, also a teacher, have three children and five grandchildren. After retirement, in 2000 Jerry and Dorothy moved back to the family ranch in Central Oregon, where they assumed the roles of "Groundskeepers Emeriti."

Ramsey's books of poems include *Love in an Earthquake* (1973), *Hand-Shadows* (1989), and *Thinking Like a Canyon: New and Selected Poems* (2012). His collection of Northwest Indian traditional stories, *Coyote Was Going There* (1977) is still in print. Since moving back to Central Oregon, he has written two books on the region's local history, *New Era* (2003) and *Words Marked by a Place* (2016), and he serves as Advisory Editor of the local history journal, *THE AGATE*. His poetry has won numerous awards, including the Lillian Fairchild Award and the Quarterly Review International Poetry Prize; and in 2017 he was given the C.E.S. Wood Award for Lifetime Achievement as an Oregon Writer.

About The Poetry Box®

The Poetry Box,® a boutique publishing company in Portland, Oregon, provides a platform for both established and emerging poets to share their words with the world through beautiful printed books and chapbooks.

Feel free to visit the online bookstore (thePoetryBox.com), where you'll find more titles including:

Tracking the Fox by Rosalie Sanara Petrouske

Elemental Things by Michael S. Glaser

Listening in the Dark by Suzy Harris

When All Else Fails by Lana Hechtman Ayers

It's a Crooked Road, but Not Far, to the House of Flowers by Wendy Erd

Earthwork by Kristin Berger

A Nest in the Heart by Vivienne Popperl

The Catalog of Small Contentments by Carolyn Martin

The Round Whisper of No Moon by Peter Kaufmann

The Hills Around Are Dust & Light by Karen Gookin

Self Dissection by Amelia Diaz Ettinger

The Call Home by Susan Johnson

Soundings by David Gonzalez

Quilting the Loose Edges by Susan Woods Morse

This Is the Lightness by Rachel Barton

and more . . .

www.ingramcontent.com/pod-product-compliance
Lightning Source LLC
LaVergne TN
LVHW050029080526
838202LV00070B/6985